PRICES! PRICES! PRICES!

Why They Go Up and Down

by **David A. Adler** • illustrated by **Edward Miller**

Holiday House / New York

Shopping malls have lots of stores. Each store has things for sale: pants, shirts, notebooks, candies, and more. And everything has a price.

Prices are important. They help you decide what to buy.

Would you pay ten cents for a small bag of pretzels? Would you pay one dollar? Would you pay fifty dollars?

The higher the price, the less likely you are to buy those pretzels.

SHIRTS

$6.00

$8.00

SALE

PANTS

$15.00

LOW PRICES

CANDY CORN

75¢

50¢

CHOCOLATE BARS

75¢

50¢

25¢

PRETZELS

PRETZELS

PRETZELS

LOLLIPOPS

35¢

35¢

Prices also help people decide what to make, grow, and sell. If people are willing to pay a high price for sneakers—a lot higher than what it costs to make them—lots of factory owners will want to make sneakers.

If the price of corn is high—a lot higher than what it costs to plant, grow, and harvest it—lots of farmers will want to grow corn.

If a store owner could sell umbrellas for a lot more than he pays for them, he would probably want to sell umbrellas.

SHOE-Mania

LOW PRICES

SALE

$40.00

$20.00

$20.00

$40.00

$30.00

$15.00

$25.00

$30.00

$25.00

$30.00

$40.00

$15.00

.00

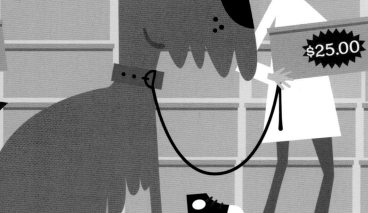

6

How are prices set?

In a marketplace where prices are free to go up and down, prices are determined by the laws of supply and demand.

Supply is how much of an item is available for sale.

Demand is how much of the item people want to buy.

A lemonade stand can teach you the laws of supply and demand.

Imagine you live on a busy corner and set up a lemonade stand. The lemonade you make is your supply. The people who want to buy a cup of your lemonade and have the money to pay for it is your demand.

Demand

Supply

For your stand, you'll need a table, tablecloth, and pitcher. You'll need those items even if you sell just one drink. You won't need more tables, tablecloths, and pitchers even if you sell one thousand drinks. The total cost of those items is called your **fixed cost**. That cost is fixed; it stays the same no matter how many drinks you sell.

$ Table
$ Tablecloth
+ $ Pitcher
──────────
$$$ Fixed Cost

$7.00

$7.00

$5.00

$8.00

$8.00

$5.00

$7.00

Tablecloths for sale

$7.00

$4.00

$7.00

$15.00

You'll also need lemons, sugar, water, and plastic cups. The more drinks you make, the more supplies you'll need. The total cost of those items is called your **variable cost**.

The variable cost per drink changes as you make more drinks.

$ Lemons
$ Sugar
$ Water
+ $ Cups
―――――――――
$$$ Variable Cost

Once you know your costs you can decide what price to charge for each drink. Surely you'll want to set the price higher than your variable cost.

On the first day, Monday morning, you make enough lemonade to fill your pitcher, enough for twenty drinks. The total cost of the lemons, sugar, water, and plastic cups is six dollars. Your variable cost per drink is thirty cents.

$1.50 Lemons
$2.00 Sugar
$1.00 Water
+ $1.50 Cups
_____
$6.00 Variable Cost

$6.00 Variable Cost
÷ 20 Drinks
_____
30¢ Variable Cost per Drink

On Monday you set the price of your lemonade at one dollar a cup.

The weather on Monday is pleasant. The demand for cold drinks is not great, but lots of people walk past your stand. By the late afternoon you have sold all twenty cups of lemonade.

Your **revenue**—the money you took in—is twenty dollars. The **variable profit**—the money left over after your variable costs have been subtracted—is fourteen dollars. You use some of that to pay your fixed costs.

Monday

$20.00 revenue
- 6.00 variable costs
$14.00 variable profit

LEMONADE $1.00

Tuesday morning you again buy supplies and make enough lemonade to fill your pitcher, enough for twenty drinks. But the weather has changed. It's very hot. You have no more lemons. You can't make more lemonade, but you know the demand for cold drinks will be great. You want to make as much money as you can, so you raise your price to two dollars. At the higher price some people decide not to buy a drink. Still, enough people are thirsty and are willing to pay two dollars for a cold drink.

On Tuesday you sell all twenty cups of lemonade. Your revenue is forty dollars. Your profit after your variable costs have been subtracted is thirty-four dollars.

You are able to pay all your fixed costs.

On Tuesday you saw that when the demand goes up but the supply remains the same prices go up. That's the first basic law of supply and demand.

LAW #1

DEMAND   PRICES

SUPPLY

LEMONADE $2.00

Wednesday morning you again make enough lemonade to fill your pitcher. But the weather has turned cold. The demand for a cold drink will not be great. Your variable cost per drink is still thirty cents. You want to sell all the lemonade you mace, so you lower your price to fifty cents.

At the lower price, even people who are not terribly thirsty buy lemonade. You sell all twenty drinks. Your revenue on Wednesday is ten dollars. Your profit is four dollars.

On Wednesday you saw that when the demand goes down but the supply remains the same prices go down. That's the second basic law of supply and demand.

Wednesday

$10.00 revenue
- 6.00 variable costs
$4.00 variable profit

LAW #2

DEMAND ↓ PRICES ↓

SUPPLY →

LEMONADE 50¢

Thursday morning the weather is pleasant. It's not too hot and not too cold. You again make enough lemonade to fill your pitcher.

You go outside and see that Julie, the girl who lives across the street, has opened her own stand. She also made a pitcher of lemonade.

The supply of cold drinks for sale on your block has increased. You don't expect more thirsty people to walk by, so the demand will not go up. You want to sell all your lemonade, so you lower the price to thirty cents.

At the lower price, even people who are not terribly thirsty buy lemonade. You sell all twenty drinks.

On Thursday it again costs you thirty cents for each drink you made. You sold each drink for thirty cents. You didn't make a profit, but you're pleased you didn't lose money.

On Thursday you saw that when the supply goes up and the demand stays the same prices go down. That's the third basic law of supply and demand.

LAW #3

SUPPLY

PRICES

DEMAND

On Friday you expect Julie to be selling lemonade. With another lemonade stand on your block it will be more difficult for you to sell drinks, so you make just enough to fill half your pitcher. But on Friday Julie doesn't set up her stand. The total supply of drinks on your block has gone down. You expect that the demand will be the same as it was the day before. You raise the price to two dollars and sell all ten drinks.

$3.00 variable cost
÷ 10 drinks
———————
30¢ variable cost per drink

SUGAR

On Friday it again costs you thirty cents for each drink you made. You sold ten drinks each for two dollars. Your revenue was twenty dollars. Your profit was seventeen dollars.

On Friday you saw that when the supply goes down and the demand stays the same prices go up. That's the fourth basic law of supply and demand.

LEMONADE $2.00

DOGHOUSE FOR SALE $17.00

Friday

$20.00 revenue
− 3.00 variable costs
$17.00 variable profit

LAW #4

SUPPLY

PRICES

DEMAND

Now you know the basic laws of supply and demand.

Now you understand why prices go up and prices go down.

Artists who lived and worked two hundred years ago created a limited number of paintings. Many museums and private collectors may be eager to have their works. When the demand goes up but the supply remains the same prices go up.

That's why the prices of some artists' works keep rising.

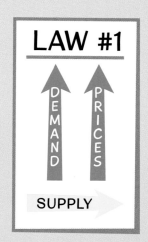

LAW #1

DEMAND   PRICES

SUPPLY

At the beginning of the summer the demand for bathing suits is high. By the end of the summer few people want to buy one. When the demand goes down but there's still plenty of supply prices go down. That's why store owners who still have bathing suits at the end of the summer will lower their prices.

END-OF-SUMMER SALE!

$8.50

$5.00

$6.59

BATHING SUITS 1/2 PRICE!

$7.00

$9.99

$6.59

END-SUMM SAL

OPEN

At the beginning of the summer watermelons are just beginning to ripen. There are not enough ripe watermelons for everyone. Later in the summer there are lots more. When the supply goes up and the demand stays the same prices go down.

That's why a slice of watermelon costs more in June than it does in August.

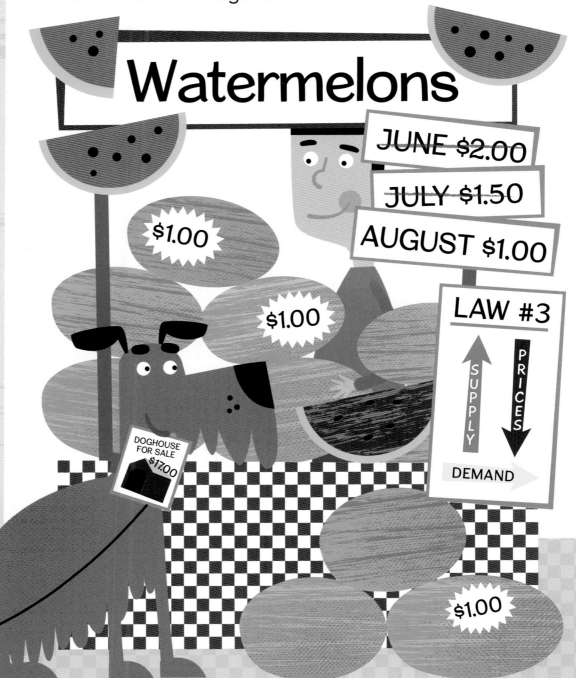

Watermelons

JUNE $2.00
JULY $1.50
AUGUST $1.00

$1.00

$1.00

$1.00

LAW #3

SUPPLY
PRICES
DEMAND

DOGHOUSE FOR SALE $17.00

From week to week people need about the same amount of gasoline to run their cars. When there is a disruption in the shipment of the oil used to make gasoline the price of gasoline will rise. When demand stays the same and the supply goes down prices go up. That's why the price of gasoline sometimes goes up.

LAW #4

SUPPLY

PRICES

DEMAND

Take a walk through a shopping mall. Look at the many signs in store windows.

Now that you know the basic laws of supply and demand, you know why prices go up and prices go down.

$3.00 $6.00 $8.00

$25.00

Mice
$1.00

Goldfish

50¢
each

Cat
Scratching
Post

$3.00

DOG
FOOD

$17.00

$3.00

DOG
FOOD

Glossary

Demand: How much of an item people are willing and able to buy

Fixed Cost: Money spent that does not change as more of an item is produced. For example, the cost to heat a bicycle factory does not increase as more bicycles are made. The heating cost is fixed.

Marketplace: Wherever goods and services are offered for sale

Profit: There is a profit whenever the money received from the sale of items is more than the total cost of producing and selling them. The difference between the money received and the costs is the profit.

Revenue: Money received from selling goods and services

Supply: How much of anything is available for sale

Variable Cost: The money spent that changes, or increases, as more of the item is produced

LAW #1

DEMAND ↑ PRICES ↑

SUPPLY →

LAW #2

DEMAND ↓ PRICES ↓

SUPPLY →

LAW #3

SUPPLY ↑ PRICES ↓

DEMAND →

LAW #4

SUPPLY ↓ PRICES ↑

DEMAND →

Laws of Supply and Demand

#1 When demand goes up but the supply remains the same prices go up.

#2 When demand goes down but the supply remains the same prices go down.

#3 When supply goes up and the demand stays the same prices go down.

#4 When supply goes down and the demand stays the same prices go up.

For Eitan J. Adler—D. A. A.

To my mom—E. M.

Text copyright © 2015 by David A. Adler
Illustrations copyright © 2015 by Edward Miller III
All Rights Reserved
HOLIDAY HOUSE is registered in the U.S. Patent and Trademark Office.
Printed and Bound in September 2020 at Tien Wah Press, Johor Bahru, Johor, Malaysia.
www.holidayhouse.com
5 7 9 10 8 6 4
Library of Congress Cataloging-in-Publication Data
Adler, David A.
Prices! Prices! Prices! : Why They Go Up and Down/ by David A. Adler ; Illustrated by Edward Miller.
pages cm
Audience: Age 6-10.
Audience: Grade 4 to 6.
ISBN 978-0-8234-3293-6 (hardcover)
1. Prices—Juvenile literature. 2. Pricing—Juvenile literature. 3. Supply and demand—Juvenile literature.
I. Miller, Edward, 1964- illustrator. II. Title.
HB221.A323 2015
338.5'2—dc23
2014017265

ISBN 978-0-8234-3574-6 (paperback)